We Go!
Buses

¡Viajamos!
En autobuses

Dana Meachen Rau

 **Marshall Cavendish**
Benchmark
New York

We go on a bus.

———❖———

Viajamos en autobús.

Buses have wheels.

Los autobuses tienen ruedas.

Buses have doors.

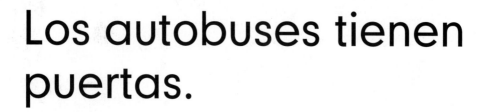

Los autobuses tienen puertas.

Buses have steps.

———❖———

Los autobuses tienen escalones.

9

Buses have drivers.

———◆———

Los autobuses tienen conductores.

Buses go on trips.

———◆———

Los autobuses van de viaje.

Buses go to camp.

Los autobuses van al campamento.

Buses go to school.

Los autobuses van a la escuela.

We go on a bus!

❖

¡Viajamos en autobús!

19

Words to Know
Palabras para aprender

camp bus
autobús de campamento

doors
puertas

driver
conductor

school bus
autobús escolar

steps
escalones

tour bus
autobús de turismo

wheels
ruedas

21

Index

Índice

About the Author

Dana Meachen Rau is the author of many other titles in the Bookworms series, as well as other nonfiction and early reader books. She lives in Burlington, Connecticut, with her husband and two children.

Sobre la autora

Dana Meachen Rau es la autora de muchos libros de la serie Bookworms y de otros libros de no ficción y de lectura para principiantes. Vive en Burlington, Connecticut, con su esposo y sus dos hijos.

With thanks to the Reading Consultants:

Nanci Vargus, Ed.D., is an Assistant Professor of Elementary Education at the University of Indianapolis.

Beth Walker Gambro is an Adjunct Professor at the University of Saint Francis in Joliet, Illinois.

Agradecemos a las asesoras de lectura:

Nanci Vargus, doctora en Educación, es profesora auxiliar de Educación Primaria en la Universidad de Indianápolis.

Beth Walker Gambro es profesora adjunta en la Universidad de Saint Francis en Joliet, Illinois.

Marshall Cavendish Benchmark
99 White Plains Road
Tarrytown, New York 10591
www.marshallcavendish.us

Library of Congress Cataloging-in-Publication Data

Rau, Dana Meachen, 1971–
[Buses. Spanish & English]
Buses = En autobuses / Dana Meachen Rau.
p. cm. — (Bookworms. We go! = ¡Viajamos!)
Includes index.
Parallel text in English and Spanish; translated from the English.
ISBN 978-0-7614-4766-5 (bilingual ed.) — ISBN 978-0-7614-4077-2 (English ed.)
1. Buses—Juvenile literature. I. Title. II. Title: Autobuses.
TL232.R35218 2010
629.28'333—dc22
2009017450

Editor: Christina Gardeski
Publisher: Michelle Bisson
Designer: Virginia Pope
Art Director: Anahid Hamparian

Spanish Translation and Text Composition by Victory Productions, Inc.
www.victoryprd.com

Photo Research by Anne Burns Images

Cover Photo by *Corbis*/Najlah Feanny

The photographs in this book are used with permission and through the courtesy of:
Alamy Images: pp. 1, 17, 20BR David R. Frazier; pp. 11, 20BL eStock Photo. *Corbis*: p. 3 Gabe Palmer;
pp. 13, 21TR Fridmar Damm/zefa. *SuperStock*: pp. 5, 15, 20TL, 21B age fotostock; pp. 7, 20TR Mauritius;
pp. 9, 21TL James J. Bissell. *Terry Wilder Stock*: p. 19.

Printed in Malaysia
1 3 5 6 4 2